George W. Bush

A Little Golden Book® Biography

By Joanna Keith
Illustrated by Jim Starr

A GOLDEN BOOK • NEW YORK

Text copyright © 2023 by Joanna Keith
Cover art and interior illustrations copyright © 2023 by Jim Starr
All rights reserved. Published in the United States by Golden Books, an imprint of Random
House Children's Books, a division of Penguin Random House LLC, 1745 Broadway,
New York, NY 10019. Golden Books, A Golden Book, A Little Golden Book, the G colophon,
and the distinctive gold spine are registered trademarks of Penguin Random House LLC.
rhcbooks.com
Educators and librarians, for a variety of teaching tools, visit us at RHTeachersLibrarians.com
Library of Congress Control Number: 2022941382
ISBN 978-0-593-64506-2 (trade) — ISBN 978-0-593-64507-9 (ebook)
Printed in the United States of America
10 9 8 7 6 5 4 3 2 1

George Walker Bush was the 43rd president of the United States of America. But long before that, he was Georgie, the oldest of six kids growing up in Midland, Texas. George was born on July 6, 1946. He was named after his father, George Herbert Walker Bush. Poppy, as his family called him, worked for a Texas oil company. George's mother was Barbara, but everyone knew her as Bar. The Bush family loved nicknames!

Young George was always on the go. He played Little League baseball and dreamed of becoming a professional player someday. He easily made friends by acting funny and telling jokes. But George could be serious, too—he ran for class president in junior high school and won!

When George turned fifteen, his parents enrolled him in boarding school. Phillips Academy was in Andover, Massachusetts, more than two thousand miles from Texas. At first George was homesick and not used to the cold New England winter. But he soon made new friends—and the best snowballs ever!

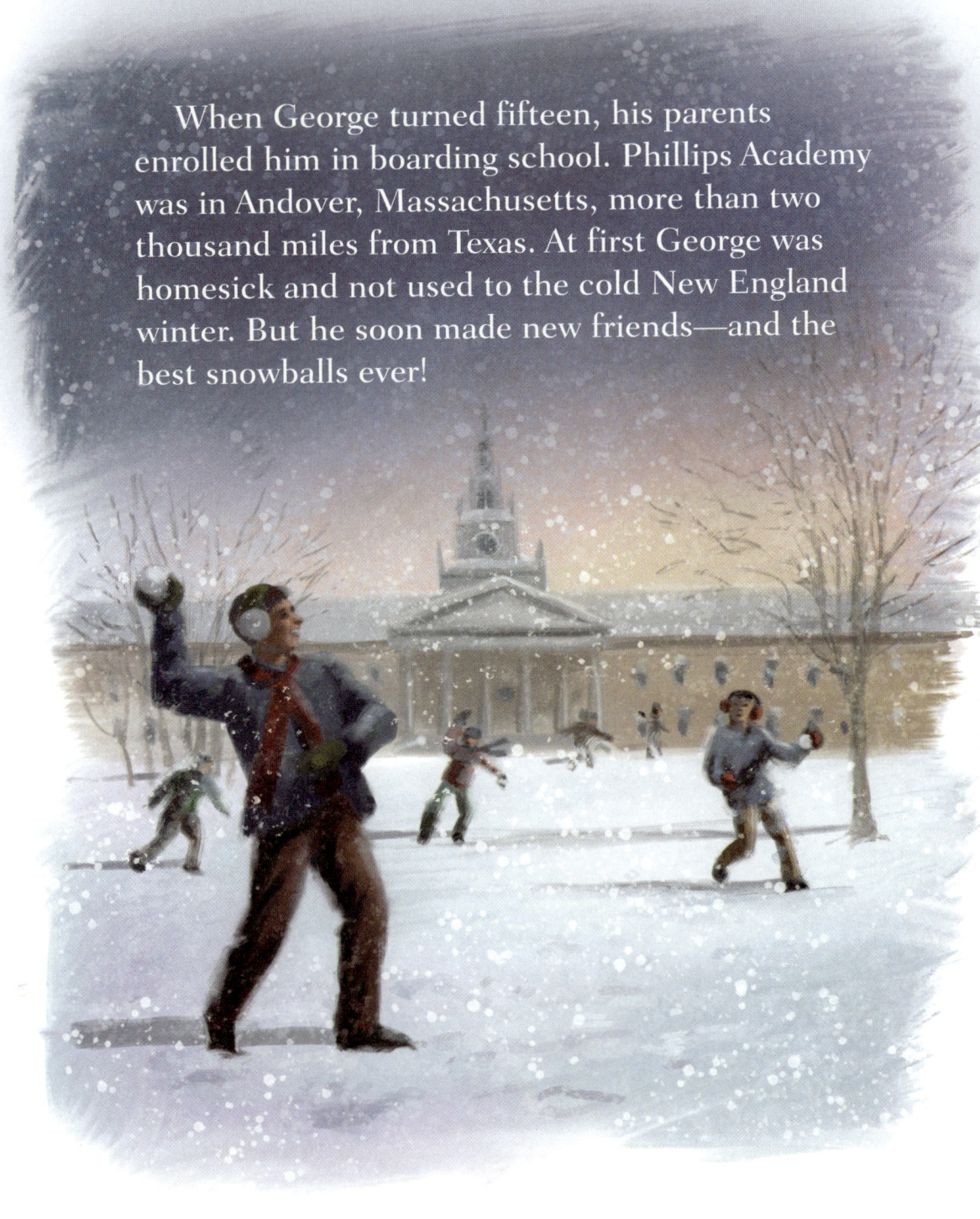

When George wasn't studying, he played baseball and basketball. One day, George decided to try something new. He became a cheerleader! Because of his great school spirit, George was made head cheerleader of the squad.

George graduated from high school and went on to Yale University, where he studied history—while some history was being made. It was the 1960s, when music and fashion were big news and astronauts rocketed to space! It was also an uneasy time in the country, as American troops were fighting a long war in Vietnam.

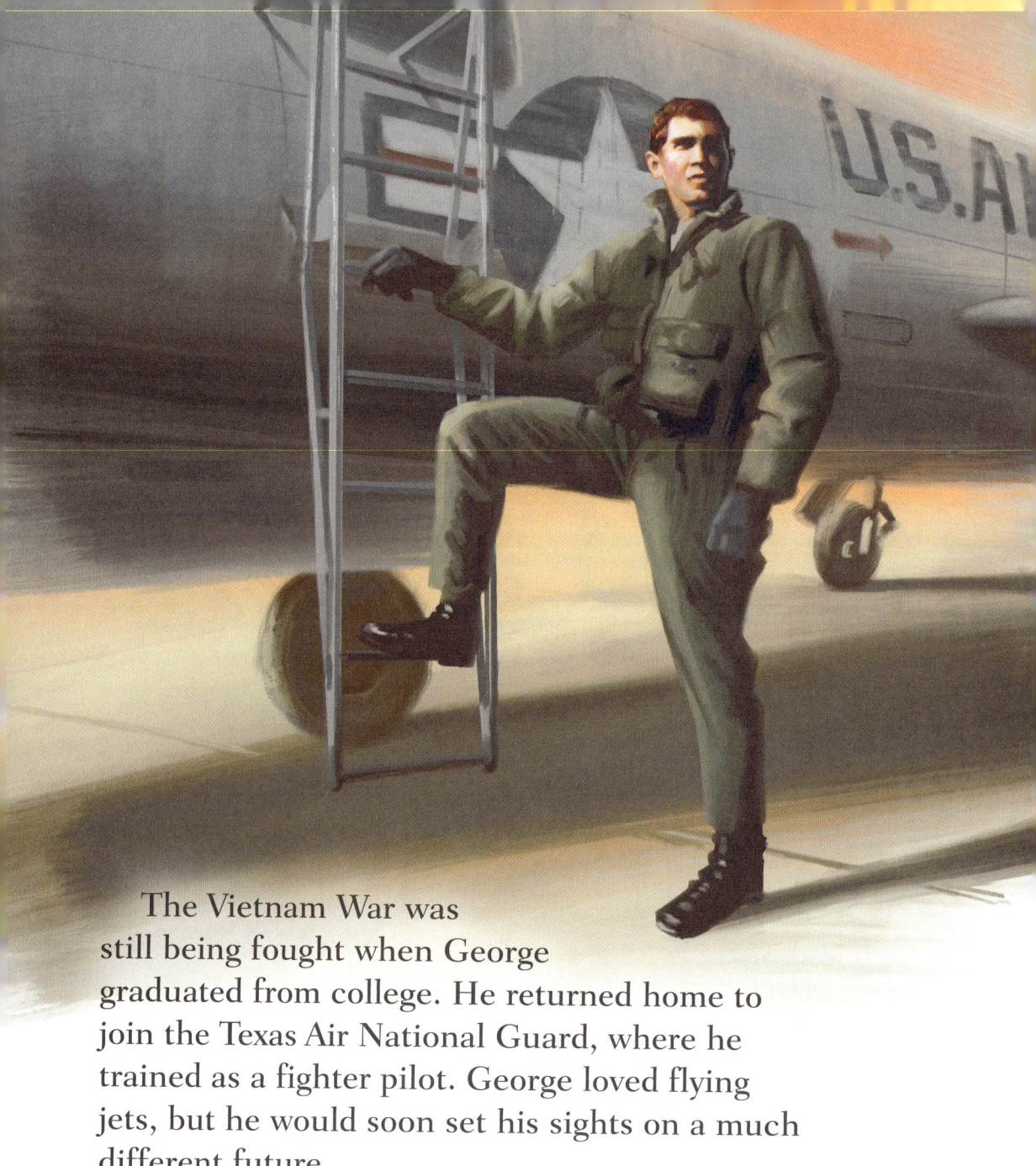

The Vietnam War was
still being fought when George
graduated from college. He returned home to
join the Texas Air National Guard, where he
trained as a fighter pilot. George loved flying
jets, but he would soon set his sights on a much
different future.

Following in his dad's footsteps, George got a job at an oil company. Texas produced the most oil in the United States, so George was in the right place.

He was in the right place again when he met Laura Welch at a friend's barbecue. George liked the friendly librarian with the bright blue eyes and asked her on a date. Three months later, they got married!

George and Laura put down roots in their home state of Texas. In November 1981, their twin girls, Barbara and Jenna, were born. Jenna was named after Laura's mom. Barbara was named after George's mom. But soon something exciting was about to happen for George's dad!

George's father had left
the oil industry to work
in politics. In 1980, he
became President Ronald
Reagan's vice president.
Eight years later, it was
Vice President Bush's
turn to run for president.

George helped his dad with the campaign,
and his hard work paid off. In November 1988,
George Herbert Walker Bush was elected the 41st
president of the United States!

Having a dad in the White House fired up George's own political dream. But he never forgot the dream he'd had since he was a kid—to play baseball. If George couldn't play professional ball, he would do the next best thing. George became co-owner of the Texas Rangers baseball team!

George loved going to the games and greeting fans, but he also still loved politics. He decided to run for Texas governor.

George won the election and kept his campaign promises. He increased school spending, and he made Texas the leading producer of wind energy in the country!

In his fourth year of office, Governor Bush decided to think even bigger. He ran for the highest office in the land—president of the United States.

The race between George and Vice President Al Gore was long and close. In the end, George Walker Bush was declared the 43rd president. George was sworn in on January 20, 2001, becoming the second son of a former U.S. president to become president. The first was John Quincy Adams—son of President John Adams.

George wasn't president for long before something terrible happened. On the morning of September 11, 2001, George was in Florida reading a storybook to a class of second graders when he received bad news.

Two planes had crashed into the Twin Towers
of the World Trade Center in New York City.
Another plane had crashed into the nation's
Pentagon in Washington, D.C. One more plane
went down in a field in Pennsylvania.

These attacks shocked the world, especially the people of New York City. George visited the site of the fallen World Trade Center. He praised the heroes of September 11—the firefighters, police officers, construction workers, and neighbors helping those in need.

George's second term as president saw another terrible event—Hurricane Katrina. The tropical storm was one of the most destructive in American history. George brought comfort to the people along the Gulf Coast. He also brought help. He signed billions of dollars in relief packages and sent thousands of National Guard troops to assist in search-and-rescue missions.

Back at the White House, George brought about more positive changes for the nation. He worked to improve schools, passed a clean-energy bill to help reduce pollution, and made medicine more affordable for America's older adults.

With all that work, George still found time to have fun. He jogged almost every day and played ball with his pups, Barney and Miss Beazley. And he enjoyed meals cooked by the White House chefs. His favorite? Cheeseburger pizza!

In 2008, President George W. Bush's second term as president came to an end. It was time for the Bush family to welcome the next First Family to the White House!

After moving back to Texas, George decided to again try something new—he learned how to paint, which he continues to do today. George enjoys painting portraits of heroes, world leaders, and even his pets.

George Walker Bush went from class president to president of the United States. Along the way, he helped people in need, solved problems, and made many friends. He also made his biggest dreams come true!